For Angela, Caryn, and JoAnne
—DAD

For my good friends,
Annette and Fred Birnbaum
—JS

LITTLE SIMON
Simon & Schuster Building, Rockefeller Center
1230 Avenue of the Americas, New York, New York 10020.
Text copyright © 1994 by Dayle Ann Dodds.
Illustrations copyright © 1994 by Jerry Smath.
LITTLE SIMON and colophon
are trademarks of Simon & Schuster.
Designed by Vicki Kalajian.
The text of this book is set in Kennerly.
The illustrations were done in watercolors with pen and ink.
Manufactured in the United States of America

10 9 8 7 6 5 4 3 2 1

Library of Congress Cataloging-in-Publication Data
Dodds, Dayle Ann. Someone is hiding / by Dayle Ann Dodds ; illustrated by
Jerry Smath. Summary: Animal characters playing the game of Sardines search
the house for the one hidden player, joining him one by one
in his hiding place as they find him. [1. Sardines
(Game)—Fiction.   2. Hide-and-seek—Fiction.   3. Animals—Fiction.
4. Stories in rhyme.   5. Counting.]   I. Smath, Jerry, ill.   II. Title.
PZ8.3.D645Sar 1994 [E]—dc20 CIP 91-24317
ISBN 0-671-75542-0

Someone
is Hiding

A LIFT-THE-FLAP COUNTING GAME

By Dayle Ann Dodds
Illustrated by Jerry Smath

LITTLE SIMON
Published by Simon & Schuster
New York   London   Toronto   Sydney   Tokyo   Singapore

Ready or not.
Look and see.
Someone is hiding.

Who can it be?

Are you...

under the table?
behind the chairs?
in the corner?
or on top of the stairs?

Peek, peek, peekaboo.
Here we come.
Where are you?

Hiding,
    hiding,
        little sardine.

Wait a minute!
Look and see.
Someone is missing....

Who can it be?

Are you...

under the rug?
in back of the plants?
in the closet with Papa's pants?

Peek, peek, peekaboo.
Now there are **2** of you,

hiding,
    hiding,
        like sardines.

Wait a minute!
Look and see.
Someone is missing....

Who can it be?

Are you...

in back of the curtains?
under the lamp?
down in the cellar, cold and damp?

Peek, peek, peekaboo.
Now there are **3** of you,

hiding,
   hiding,
      like sardines.

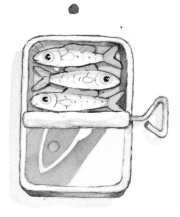

Wait a minute!
Look and see.
Someone is missing....

Who can it be?

Are you...

in the cupboard?
behind the cookie jar?
We all know you can't be far!

Peek, peek, peekaboo.
Now there are 4 of you,

hiding,
   hiding,
      like sardines.

Wait a minute!
Look and see.
Someone is missing....

Who can it be?

Are you…

under the piano?
behind the couch?
Sshh!
Listen!

Did someone say *ouch*?

Peek, peek, peekaboo.
Now there are **5** of you,

hiding,
　　hiding,
　　　　like sardines.

Wait a minute!
Look and see.
Someone is missing....

Who can it be?

Are you...

in the attic?
behind the trunk,
dusty and musty and full of junk?

Peek, peek, peekaboo.
Now there are **6** of you,

hiding,
 hiding,
  like sardines.

Wait a minute!
Look and see.
If EVERYONE is missing,

that just leaves...

Was that a giggle?
Was that a squeak?

Quietly, quietly,
take a peek....

PEEK, PEEK, PEEKABOO!
I FOUND ALL OF YOU,
HIDING,
     HIDING,
          LIKE SARDINES.

Christopher
from
Nana
'97